BOOK 1

A CHILDREN'S HISTORY OF
GRAND MARAIS, MINNESOTA

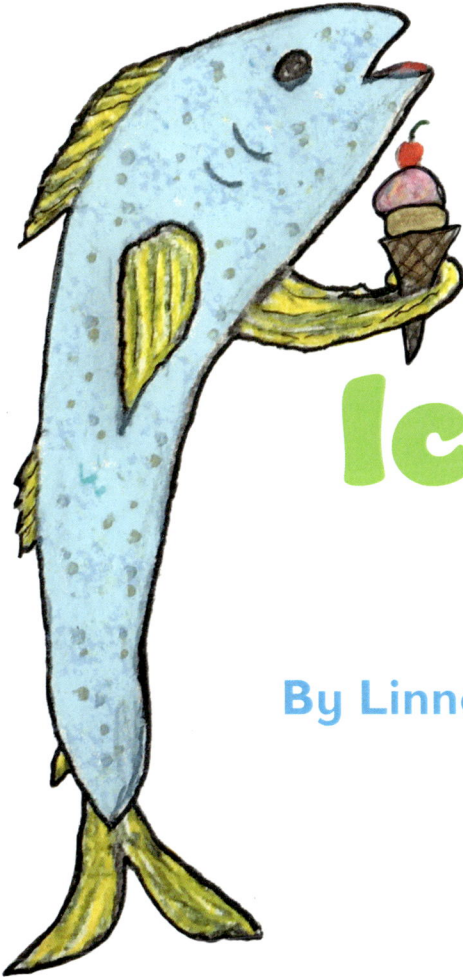

Ice Cream and Fish illustration by Linnea Ljosenvoor

Ice Cream & Fish

By Linnea Ljosenvoor and Iris Works

MINNeSota
CHILDREN'S PRESS
WWW.MINNCHILDPRESS.ORG

Produced in creative collaboration with Editor and Publisher
Anne Brataas of Minnesota Children's Press.

Design and Layout by Brittany Lynk

MINNeSOTa
CHILDREN'S PRESS
WWW.MINNCHILDPRESS.ORG

The mission of **Minnesota Children's Press** is to mentor the writing and illustration skills of rural students ages 5-15 for the purpose of revealing and amplifying voices of those seldom heard in society — yet who bear the full, long burden of the future that adults make today. Through children's inborn creative caring, exuberant problem-solving, and heroic imaginings, Minnesota Children's Press co-creates joyful, positive stories of community to unite and guide us to a generative future.

As award-winning curriculum designers, Minnesota Children's Press developed an entrepreneurial Story Scouts® model and proprietary production method: Co-Co Books® — co-creative collaborations. Children are paired with communication professionals who mentor them to jointly produce words, pictures, and stories that children sell to raise money for civic betterment projects the children identify. In the process, each Story Scout creates a personal college-ready and career-relevant portfolio of achievement, intellectual ambition, community service, confident competencies — and joyful, collaborative work ethic!

All Minnesota Children's Press Books are written, illustrated, published, and printed in the United States.

First published by Minnesota Children's Press, 2020.

10 9 8 7 6 5 4 3 2

This book was typeset in Congenial.
Illustrations were done in mixed media, with select digital editing and enhancements.

ISBN: 978-0-9978731-9-1 • Library of Congress Control Number: 2020918983

Dedication

"We were poor in money, but rich in food, family, and friends."

— Gordon Lindquist, 4 August 2020,
in an outdoor, masked interview with Iris and Linnea

L–R: Joyce and Gordon Lindquist, Bob and Bev Pratt

With deepest gratitude and respect, this book is dedicated to the late Bob Pratt of Grand Marais, his wife Bev Pratt, and their lifelong mentoring and teaching friends, Gordon and Joyce Lindquist. All make Grand Marais a better place to live.

Together, these families made powerful differences in so many Cook County lives. Now 90, the Lindquists inspire us in 2020 through the stories they share about the resiliency, resourcefulness, and "riches" they experienced following the stock market crash of 1929 that began the Great American Depression. Gordon Lindquist expressed their riches as the food they caught, hunted, grew, and shared, and the family and friends they cared for as children in the American Depression 1929–1939. It was this commitment to caring that shaped the character and identity of Cook County, and which we strive to enliven with these stories and pictures to help guide children of Cook County into a bright and stable future.

We thank them all for the inspiration and hope they provide us, as children in the Pandemic Recession of 2020.

About this Co-Co Book

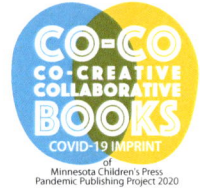

Co-Co Books is a creative, community-building, youth-nurturing communication response to the global coronavirus pandemic of 2020. Minnesota Children's Press created this special imprint and logo in March 2020 after public health stay-at-home orders were issued to contain the spread of the pandemic. We are an artistic intervention in disrupted youth development. It is our means of coping with and surmounting the pandemic challenges to hope, unity, and mental health. We choose to meet these challenges with creativity and originality, while living in sympathy with each other, striving to promote just and generative well-being.

CO-CO
CO-CREATIVE COLLABORATIVE BOOKS
COVID-19 IMPRINT
of
Minnesota Children's Press
Pandemic Publishing Project 2020

Contributors

Poster Parade Artists
Kindergarten – 4th Grade

Ari
Emily
Kian
Leah
Leo
Logan
Lucas

Marlo
Mavis
Odin
Parker
Runa
Sabrina
Tib

Book Camp Authors, Illustrators, Copy Editors, & Proofreaders
5th – 7th Grade

In Person
Linnea L.
Iris W.

Remote
Lily C.
Maddy M.

Stick Figure Artist & Mentor

Kip Hathaway

Timeline Illustrator & Youth Copy Desk Chief
10th Grade

Sammie Garrity

Primary Historical Interview Sources

Gordon and Joyce Lindquist
David Leng
Bob Pratt, April 2018

Special Thanks to Outstanding Community Collaborators

We are grateful for a generous grant from the Lloyd K. Johnson Foundation of Duluth; to Cook County History Museum archives and curators; to youth Story Scouts participants and adult leaders from the Cook County YMCA and Cook County Community Education; generous grants from Minnesota Children's Press donors who helped us rent a well-ventilated, spacious indoor studio for writing and illustrating when inhospitable weather prevented productive outdoor work. To all who helped us along the way, thank you!

Table of Contents

Outdoor Book Camp (www.minnchildpress.org/book-camp) kids produced Parts I & II of Ice Cream & Fish, guided by Minnesota Children's Press adult mentors in a 10-day Outdoor Book Camp.

Outdoor Book Camp took place on the porches, lawns, playgrounds, rocks, shallows, and shoreline of Lake Superior in Grand Marais, Minnesota, — an outside classroom — to ensure we always created in coronavirus-safe spaces with lots of fresh air, ample room for children to separate from each other — and play! — while being in proximity to collaborate on a book. Face coverings were mandatory outdoors if physical distance could not be maintained, as was frequent hand sanitizing, use of individual bins with pencils and art materials. Each child was assigned their own keyboard and iPad to eliminate cross-contamination from sharing of materials.

Part III illustrations were produced by 15 children in grades K-4 in a collaboration with the Cook County YMCA Kids' Camp. We organized a poster-parade of kindness signs the children conceived in Minnesota Children's Press' empathy writeshop of "staffing" an injured stuffed-animal hospital. Next, we painted the feelings and sayings discovered in our empathy writeshop of healing the stuffed animals. Then we marched our large printed posters over to our local Care Center. Showing residents our signs through their windows kept everyone safe from contagion, and made us all feel happy and connected!

Happy and connected — that's a major goal of Outdoor Book Camp. We also offered creative purpose and achievement. We aimed to preserve for children that familiar sense of outdoors summer wonder and release by providing them with healthy, creative, active summer experiences of positive and purposeful socialization through peer interactions — all outside.

As we believe this book shows, Outdoor Book Camp is a successful creative inquiry-based learning prototype involving four children in grades 5-7, and 15 children in grades K-4. Given Cook County's Norwegian heritage, Outdoor Book Camp is a perfect fit for us because it embodies the Norwegian cultural concept of friluftsliv — free air life.

Part I:
A Child's Illustrated History

Visual Timeline of ~200 Years of Grand Marais Area Economic History, 1823–2020

by Sammie Garrity, 10th Grader

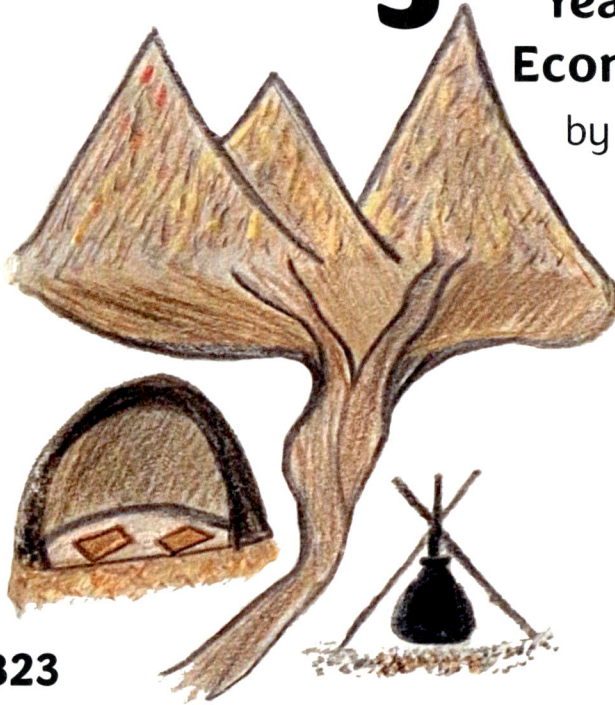

1823

ANISHINAABEG TERRITORY

FUR TRADE

The village now called Grand Marais was named Gitchi Bitobig, and was more of a trading campground than a permanent residence.

1850s

1854 Treaty of LaPointe cedes Indian Lands

FISH, EXPLORATION: lumber, silver, copper

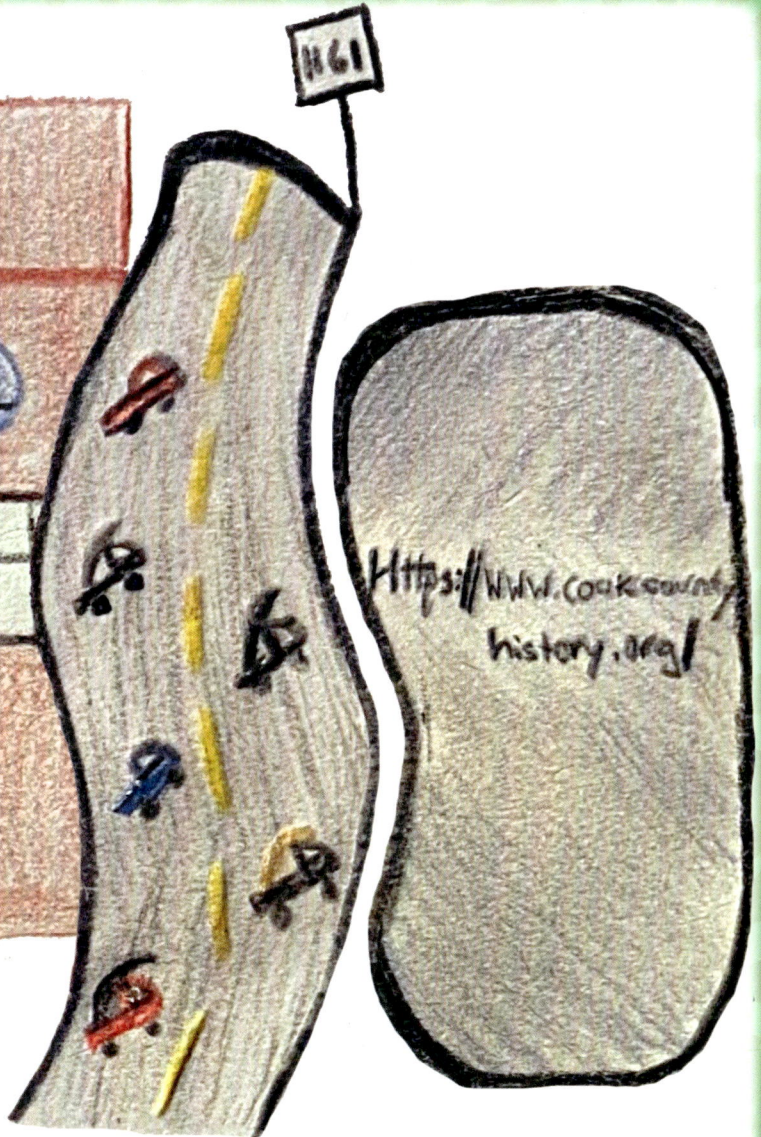

1880s
LUMBER, FISH

1920s
ROADS & AUTOMOBILE
TOURISM, ARTS CULTURE

2000s
21ST CENTURY
INTERNET TOURISM

2

Part II:
Ice Cream

A History of Grand Marais Ice Cream Stores

by Iris Works, 5th Grader

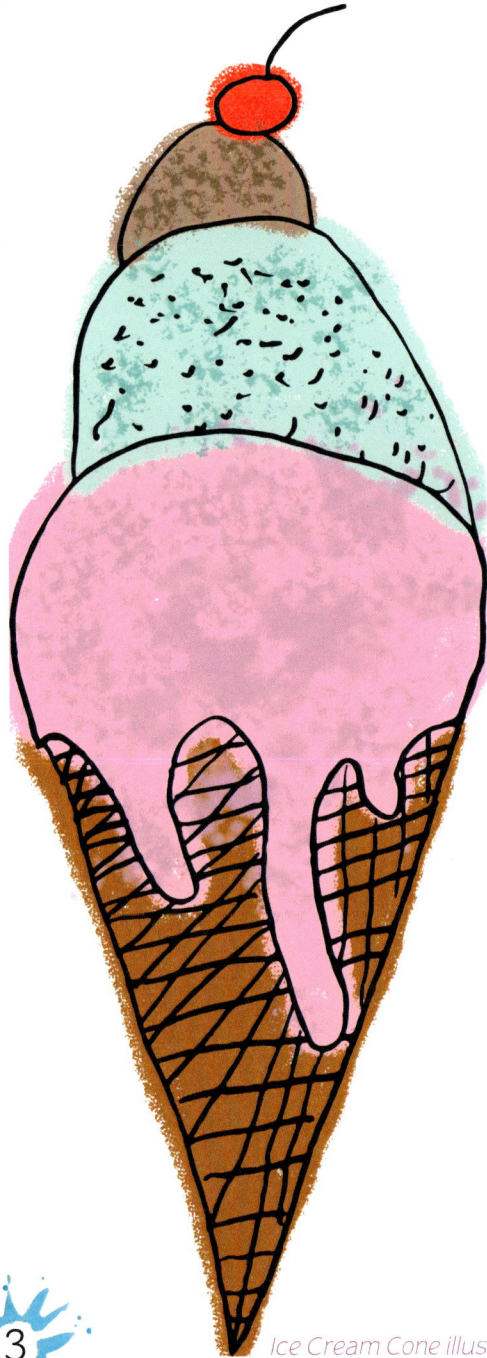

Editor's Note: An invitation to imagine from Linnea:

It's a hot summer day in Grand Marais, Minnesota, in 1938. You are walking down the street with five nickels jangling in your pocket. You feel rich! As you go past the barbershop you decide you can spare one nickel for an ice cream cone. You walk over to the Grand Marais Ice Cream Store, on the corner of where the Joynes Department Store is now. As you walk in, you hear chattering from other kids in the ice cream shop happily enjoying ice cream and potato chips. As you walk up to the counter you have a delicious decision to make. What do you want: chocolate or vanilla?

Ice Cream Cone illustration by Iris Works

In the 1930s, there were two ice cream stores open at the same time in Grand Marais, and they were about one block from each other on Wisconsin Street. The first one was called the Grand Marais Ice Cream Store. It was located in a building called the Soderberg Building that got moved a bunch of times, and was owned by Ruth Soderberg. The Soderberg Building was a big deal in downtown Grand Marais then. When the ice cream store was there, it was located where Joynes Department Store is. When it was located at the corner of Wisconsin and West 1st Avenue, Ruth supplied ice cream to other cafes, served cones and dishes of it, and also sold homemade potato chips, pies, and coffee, according to Gordon Lindquist, who moved to Grand Marais in 1930 when he was just a few months old. He is a primary source for the history of ice cream in Grand Marais because he actually went to the stores, ate the ice cream, and remembers that the Grand Marais Ice Cream Store served just vanilla or chocolate ice cream — no other flavors or sprinkles, and that cones were five cents, which was a lot of money then.

Grand Marais Main Street illustration by Iris Works

Mr. Lindquist lived on a gravel road above town, at the edge of town before County Road 7 or the YMCA were built. There was nothing. Just woods. He always liked to go to the Grand Marais Ice Cream Store and also, to the Leng's Soda Fountain one block east of it.

Mr. Lindquist said most people thought the Leng's Soda Fountain was a little more friendly — Ruth Soderberg was strict, just like her sister, Olga, who was Mr. Lindquist's school librarian. "You had to mind your manners," is how Mr. Lindquist remembers time in Olga Soderberg's school library. We found this historical picture (Photo 1, below) of the Grand Marais Ice Cream Store in 1933 at the Cook County History Museum, which is really cool.

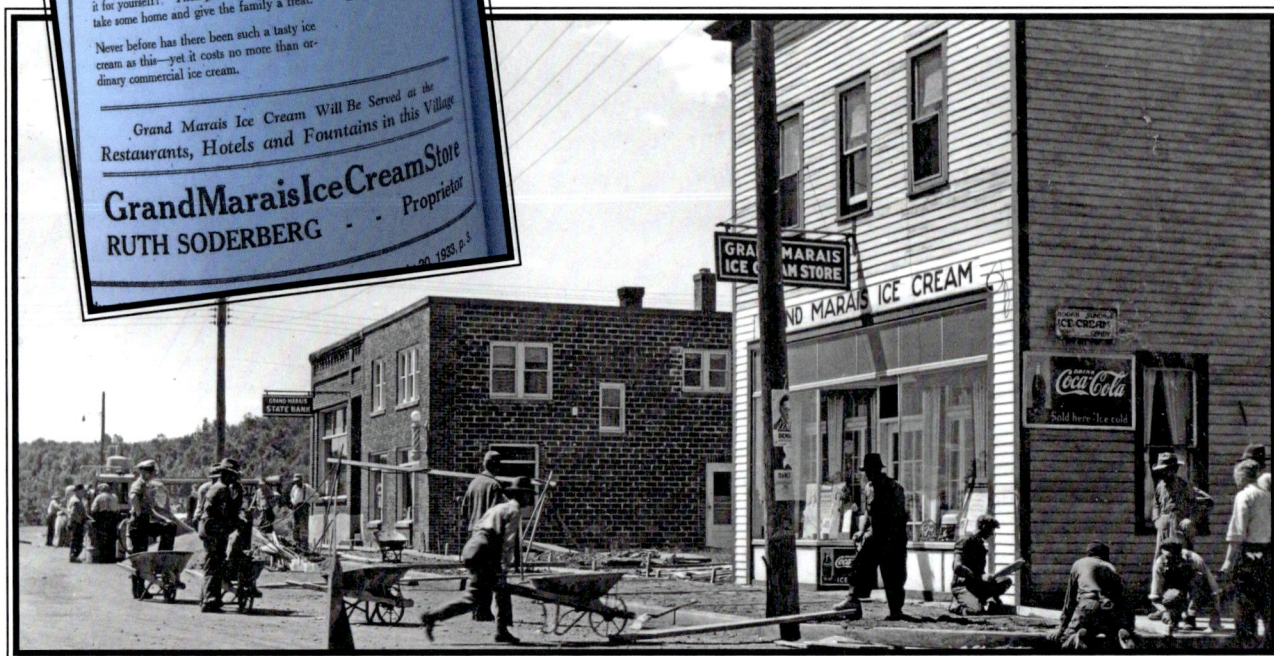

Announcing
Our Own
Grand Marais Ice Cream
The Richest and Finest Ever Made

Our freezer installation is the new and improved method of producing the finest, richest and tastiest ice cream ever known. We cordially invite you to come in and see us freeze this delicious ice cream.

You'll say it's the most delicious ice cream you ever tasted—and you'll come back for more—again and again. Because it's the richest and finest ever made.

Frozen fresh at frequent intervals right before your eyes. Rich, creamy, velvety beyond compare—flavor that tickles your palate all the way down—our new *Grand Marais* Ice Cream surely hits the spot.

But there's really only one way to find out about it—and that's to come in and sample it for yourself! Then you'll surely want to take some home and give the family a treat.

Never before has there been such a tasty ice cream as this—yet it costs no more than ordinary commercial ice cream.

You are Invited...

Anyone who has not as yet been in our store is invited to come in and sample our Ice Cream.

Children Must be Accompanied by their parents.

Price-One Quart 50 Cents

Grand Marais Ice Cream Will Be Served at the Restaurants, Hotels and Fountains in this Village

GrandMaraisIceCreamStore
RUTH SODERBERG - - Proprietor

During the Depression of the 1930s, Grand Marais' early entrepreneur Ruth Soderberg opened the first ice cream store in town: the Grand Marais Ice Cream Store. The picture above shows its storefront on Wisconsin Street, near where the modern Joynes Department Store is located. · SOURCE: Cook County History Museum

People liked Leng's because it offered more items, such as a green river drink, which was a kind of green fizzy sweet drink. But then, there were Ruth Soderberg's homemade potato chips at the Grand Marais Ice Cream Store, and people thought those were great. Leng's also had a big magazine and comic book section at the back of the store. That was a big draw for kids. Remember, there were no TVs then, or computers or iPhones. But in 1930s in Grand Marais, there were two (!) movie theaters: the Shore, on the empty lot next to the modern

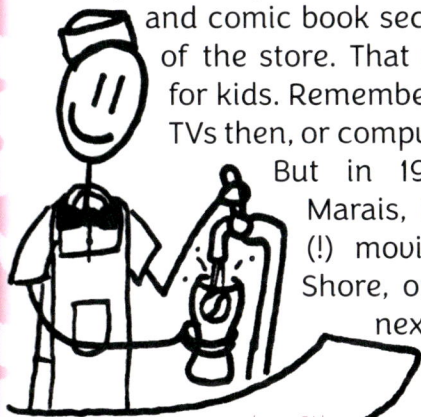

Stick figure by Kip Hathaway

6

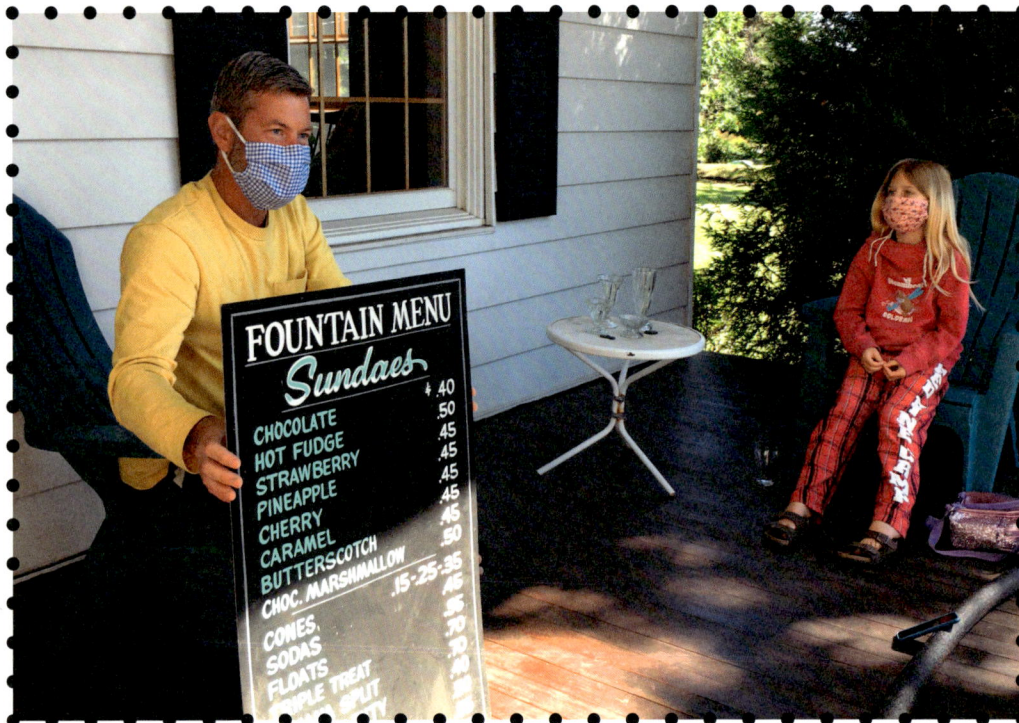

Left: Outdoor Book Camp Story Scout Iris Works interviews David Leng, who is newly returned to Grand Marais from Brooklyn, New York, with his family.

David is the grandson of the original Leng's Soda Fountain family owners, Earl and Ethyl. Here he displays an original Leng's menu from the heyday of ice cream heaven once found at Leng's shop.

CREDIT: Minnesota Children's Press

FOUNTAIN MENU
Sundaes

	$ .40
	.50
CHOCOLATE	.45
HOT FUDGE	.45
STRAWBERRY	.45
PINEAPPLE	.45
CHERRY	.45
CARAMEL	.50
BUTTERSCOTCH	
CHOC. MARSHMALLOW	.15-.25-.35
CONES	
SODAS	
FLOATS	

Blue Water Cafe; and the Wigwam, located by where the Grand Marais Library is now, where the Gunflint Arch with the Bear and Canoe signs are.

ICE CREAM 5¢

We got to interview another primary source, too: David Leng, the grandson of Earl Leng, who owned Leng's Soda Fountain.

Mr. Earl Leng seems like a great and fun grandpa because David said one of his favorite things about visiting his grandpa was going to the Leng's Soda

Stick figure by Kip Hathaway

Fountain at night, after it had closed, and his grandpa would say: "Make whatever you want!" So he would just pile on the ice cream and toppings. There were so many to pick from, and special dishes for serving each one in. After his grandfather sold the store, another family operated it for awhile, but it closed in 1989. We all want it to come back!

It turns out they had a lot of ice cream in old Grand Marais — and a lot of fish. It was the Depression of the 1930s, a time a little like ours because people had trouble finding work. They did not have the coronavirus then though.

But life was hard. Mr. Lindquist remembers that most people had to work really hard, and help each other to get by — "but we were happy. We didn't know we were poor because everybody was. There was no one to compare yourself to who might be so much better off."

And I want to put this in the story, this quote that he said, because it sounds nice and it does mean a bunch of things: "We were poor in money, but rich in food."

Every family fished, hunted, baked, and raised garden vegetables. Mr. Lindquist said his family ate venison and fish all year that his mother canned. To make the venison less dry, he said she mixed it with pig fat — they raised pigs, too. And the cool thing is that they put pig fat and venison together in Mason jars for more flavor.

For school, all kids went to kindergarten for the first time in the 1953 because his wife, Joyce Russell Lindquist, went to college at the University of Minnesota in Duluth to learn how to be a kindergarten teacher and she actually started the first kindergarten in Cook County! Her students were from Tofte,

Above: Outdoor Book Camp Story Scout Linnea Ljosenvoor interviews primary sources Joyce and Gordon Lindquist to learn about early days of kindergarten.

CREDIT: Minnesota Children's Press

Left: Joyce started Grand Marais' first kindergarten.

SOURCE: Cook County History Museum

Schroeder, Lutsen, and Grand Marais. And the classes were huge! She taught 50 kids in the morning, and 50 kids in the afternoon — all by herself. "You had to be really organized or it wouldn't work," she said. So every day she came prepared with a story, a song, a craft — naps were required — and maybe a worksheet or art project.

The cottages that Mrs. Lindquist's family rented opened in 1948. But they were built earlier. The were once known as The Birches. When her father, Robert Russell, bought the cottages he renamed them "Russell's Cottages."

At Book Camp, one of the things we learn is how to proof read and copy edit so there aren't mistakes. So when you do this to the name of the cottages, it seems like there is a man named Russell, because of the apostrophe placement, showing it is singular. Just one Russell. But the family owned it, so it probably should be Russells' Cottages if they wanted people to know that. I guess they didn't. ∎

Below: Gordon Lindquist caught this 36 pound lake trout in about 1947, just as the parasitic sea lamprey were devastating lake trout. Today, this kind of catch while fishing offshore from the Grand Marais harbor is nearly impossible to imagine. Back then, Mr. Lindquist said it wasn't unusual to catch 100 pounds of lake trout "three or four pretty good in size" in four hours. No wonder he still keeps this photo on his office wall!

SOURCE: Gordon Lindquist

Above: Outdoor Book Camp Story Scouts illustrate and write in one of the Russell's Cottages.

CREDIT: Minnesota Children's Press

Grand Marais Ice Cream illustration by Linnea Ljosenvoor

Illustrator's Note:

Even though our research shows the Grand Marais Ice Cream Store did not have a candy counter, I wish it did. In a candy counter I would include such things as gum, chocolate bars, taffy, lollipops, gummy worms, gummy bears, licorice, circus peanuts, lemon drops and those candy Legos I got at that one candy store once. I also picture it a light pink, for some reason.

Part III:
Fish

A History of Grand Marais Lake Trout & Sea Lamprey

by Linnea Ljosenvoor, 7th Grader

Editor's Note: *During the 1900s, Grand Marais was an important center of the North Shore fishing and logging industries. It added tourism to its economy as roads were built and cars improved. In the 1920s, fishermen started renting out their fishing huts to tourists, and many of those small, lakeside cabins still exist. The first inhabitants of the area, the Anishinaabeg Native peoples, were originally self-sufficient. Later they trapped and traded furs and fish with early settlers. In this story, we focus on our primary source historical interview with Gordon Lindquist to explore the actual history he lived and the importance of two special fish in Grand Marais' history.*

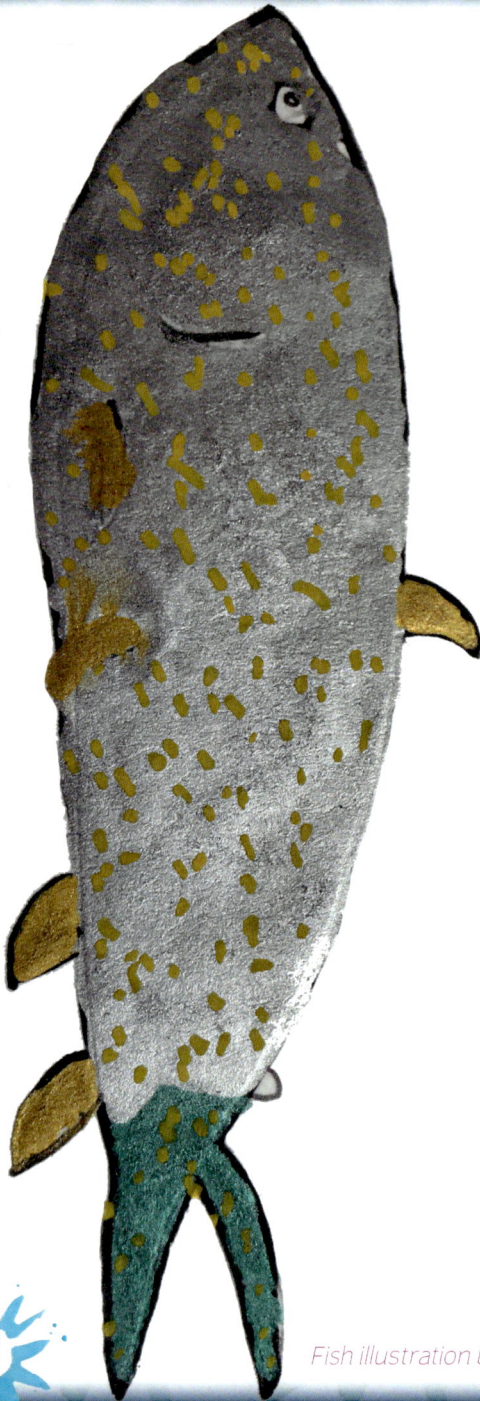

Fish illustration by Iris Works

Grand Marais native Gordon Lindquist is 90 years old and he clearly remembers the shock of the first time that he saw a sea lamprey attached to a lake trout. It was in the 1950s, and he was in his early 20s. He had fished for lake trout nearly his whole life. But on that day, he reeled in a monstrous vision. It was something he'd never seen before: a sea lamprey. It was a fish that changed life on Lake Superior.

"Before the arrival of the sea lamprey, we used to go right off the shore here and catch 100 pounds of lake trout in a day, maybe three or four fish," Mr. Lindquist said in August 2020 in an interview with Book Camp Story Scouts. Since it was the coronavirus pandemic times, even though we were all healthy, we were sitting 6-10 feet apart, outdoors on Mr. Lindquist's deck, with all of us wearing cloth face coverings so wouldn't spread any germs.

Mr. Lindquist explained that a sea lamprey is a jawless, parasitic fish that resembles an eel. It is an invasive species brought into Lake Superior from Great Lakes' ship's ballast. Lampreys kill lake trout by attaching their suction cup mouths lined with teeth to lake trout and using razor-sharp tongues to suck the blood and fluids out of them (see my illustration). That's why they are nicknamed "the vampire fish of the Great Lakes".

At the Cook County History Museum, we found a news article from March 20, 1947, announcing the dangerous arrival of sea lamprey in Lake Superior. Over the next years, sea lamprey not only killed lake trout, they killed an entire fishing industry that so many North Shore fishermen relied on.

The first lamprey Mr. Lindquist saw was about a foot long. It dangled from the side of the lake trout he caught. According to Mr. Lindquist, he could detach the lamprey from the lake trout by pressing on the back of the lamprey's head with his thumb. Then he placed the sea lamprey in a 5 gallon bucket, and it attached its suction cup mouth to the bottom of the bucket! That meant Mr. Lindquist could actually lift the bucket up by grabbing the lamprey's creepy body like a handle!

When lamprey attacked lake trout the trout would have scars where the lamprey's mouth attached (see my picture of the wound.) A lamprey mouth has circular rows of teeth, with a super sharp tongue in the middle they use to pierce fish skin. Once a lamprey attached, the lake trout would scrape against the rocks to try and get the lamprey off, Mr. Lindquist explained. If the lake

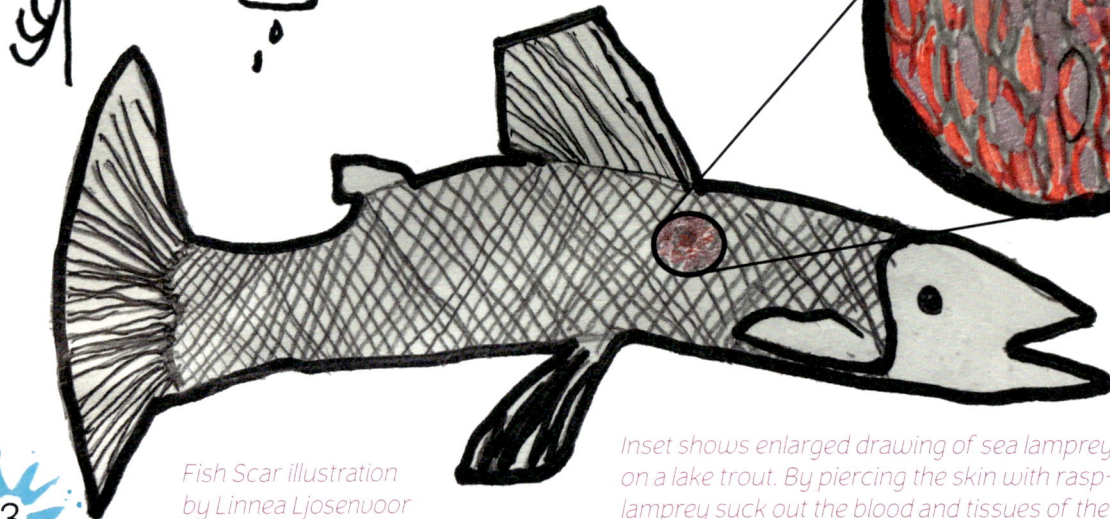

Stick figures by Kip Hathaway

40 lbs

Fish Scar illustration by Linnea Ljosenvoor

Inset shows enlarged drawing of sea lamprey wound on a lake trout. By piercing the skin with rasp-like teeth lamprey suck out the blood and tissues of the fish.

A LAKE-FRONT SCENE AT GRAND MARAIS, M

Fish and fishing — both lake trout and herring — were an important part of Grand Marais' early economy and identity in the late 1800s and early-mid 1900s.

SOURCE: Cook County History Museum

trout survived the lamprey attack and got rid of the lamprey, fishermen like Mr. Lindquist would catch them and find scars all over the fish bodies. "It was very common from the '50s on to catch scarred lake trout — if you could catch any at all. The lamprey almost destroyed them all," he said sadly.

But he also explained that the lake trout started to come back in Lake Superior after scientists developed a milk-colored chemical that they released into streams where young lamprey live before swimming into Lake Superior. It killed lamprey, but supposedly, not other things. Lake trout populations are healthier today. Still, controlling sea lampreys is a constant problem.

Sea lampreys do not bother herring because herring have heavier scales than lake trout, and the lamprey cannot get past those scales, Mr. Lindquist said. Fishermen who fished for herring were called "herring chokers" as a nickname because to get them out of the nets, they had to grab — "choke" — them by the gills. But that is a fish story for another day! ∎

14

Part IV:
Poster Parade Project

by Kindergarten – 4th Graders

Ari	Logan	Parker
Emily	Lucas	Runa
Kian	Marlo	Sabrina
Leah	Mavis	Tib
Leo	Odin	

Bloom! We See You!
by Tib

Outdoor Book Camp took place in August 2020 on the porches, lawns, playgrounds, rocks, shallows, and shoreline of Lake Superior in Grand Marais, Minnesota, to ensure we always created in coronavirus-safe spaces with lots of fresh air, ample room for children to separate from each other – and play! · CREDIT: Minnesota Children's Press

Poster Parade Project illustrations were produced by 15 children in grades K–4 in a collaboration with the Cook County YMCA Kids' Camp. We organized a poster-parade of kindness signs the children conceived in Minnesota Children's Press' empathy writeshop of "staffing" an injured stuffed-animal hospital. Next, we painted the feelings and sayings discovered in our empathy writeshop of healing the stuffed animals. Then we marched our large printed posters over to our local Care Center. Showing residents our signs through their windows kept everyone safe from contagion, and made us all feel happy and connected!

Colored Kisses to You!
by Leah
Credit: ©2020 Art by Leah. ©2020 Production by Minnesota Children's Press. All Rights Reserved.

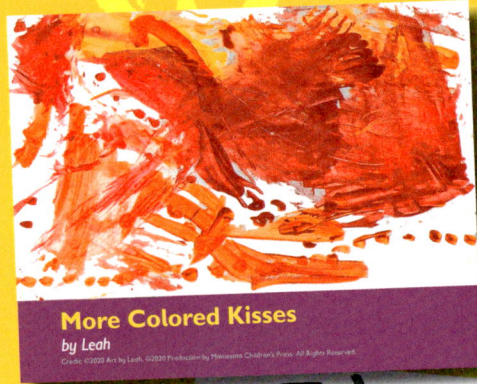
More Colored Kisses
by Leah
Credit: ©2020 Art by Leah. ©2020 Production by Minnesota Children's Press. All Rights Reserved.

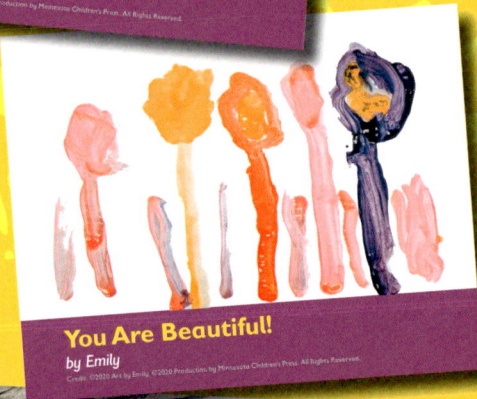
You Are Beautiful!
by Emily
Credit: ©2020 Art by Emily. ©2020 Production by Minnesota Children's Press. All Rights Reserved.

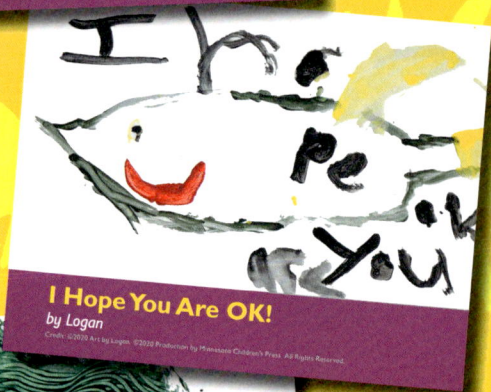
I Hope You Are OK!
by Logan
Credit: ©2020 Art by Logan. ©2020 Production by Minnesota Children's Press. All Rights Reserved.

Water and Fish Say, "Let's Play!
by Ari

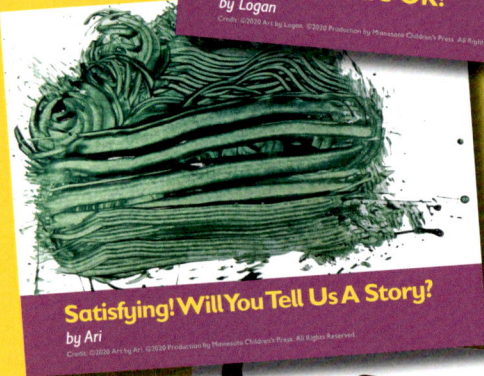
Satisfying! Will You Tell Us A Story?
by Ari
Credit: ©2020 Art by Ari. ©2020 Production by Minnesota Children's Press. All Rights Reserved.

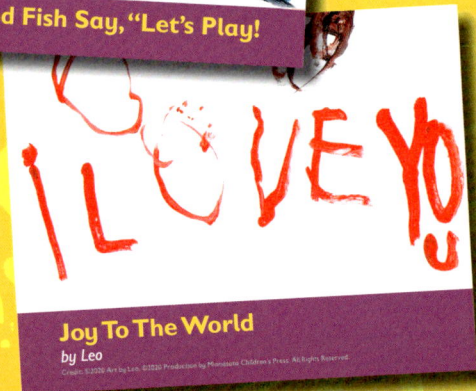
Joy To The World
by Leo
Credit: ©2020 Art by Leo. ©2020 Production by Minnesota Children's Press. All Rights Reserved.

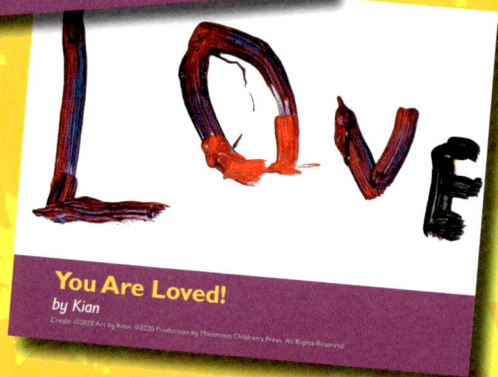
You Are Loved!
by Kian
Credit: ©2020 Art by Kian. ©2020 Production by Minnesota Children's Press. All Rights Reserved.

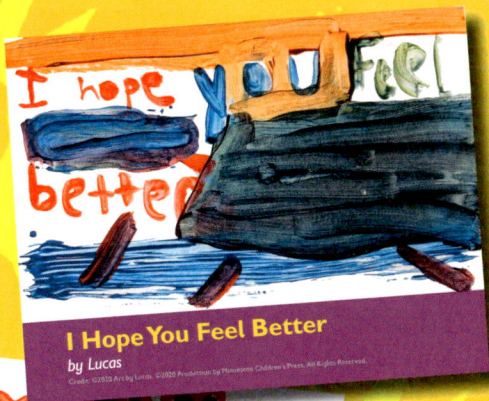
I Hope You Feel Better
by Lucas

Let the Light Shine!
by Marlo

We Miss You!
by Mavis

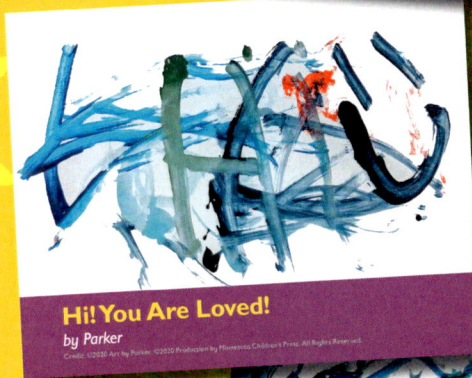
Hi! You Are Loved!
by Parker

Good and Nice!
by Odin

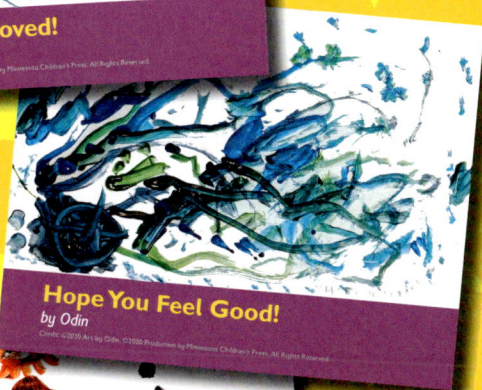
Hope You Feel Good!
by Odin

Happy! I Love!
by Runa

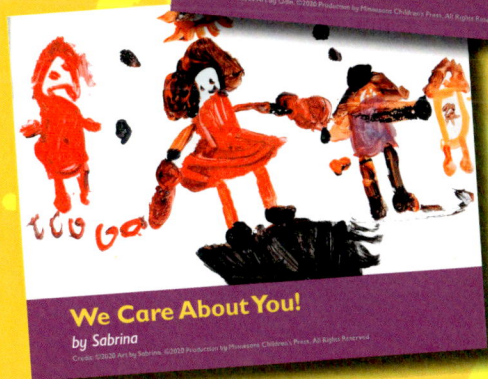
We Care About You!
by Sabrina

Part V:
How We Did It

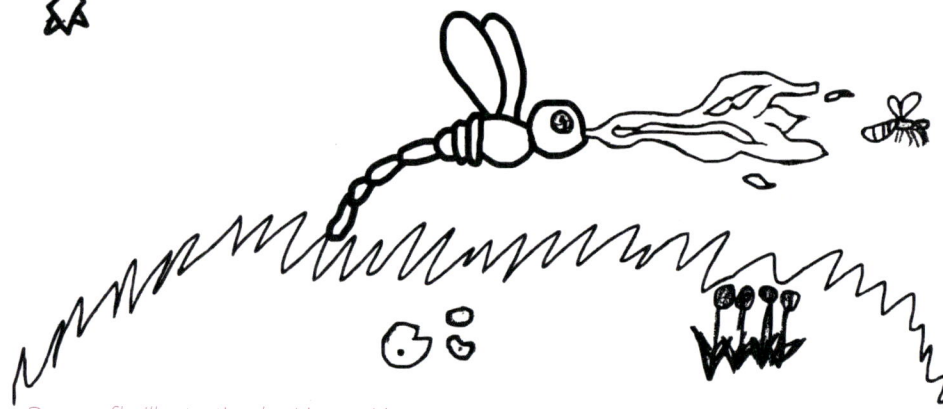

OUR METHOD: We researched our stories by conducting outdoor primary source interviews with community members Gordon and Joyce Lindquist, and by visiting the Cook County History Museum. Thank you!

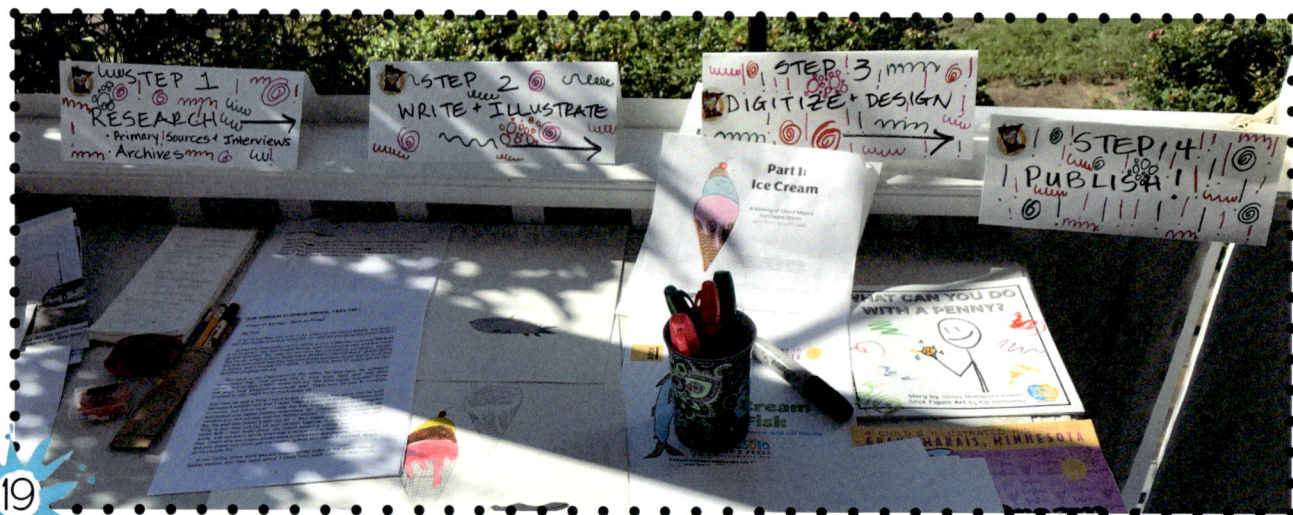

Dragonfly illustration by Linnea Ljosenvoor

STEP 1 RESEARCH
Primary Sources + Interviews
Archives

STEP 2 WRITE + ILLUSTRATE

STEP 3 DIGITIZE + DESIGN

STEP 4 PUBLISH!

Part I: Ice Cream

WHAT CAN YOU DO WITH A PENNY?

STEP 1
RESEARCH →
• Primary Sources + Interviews
• Archives

Gordon Lindquist talks to Story Scout Linnea about fishing in Lake Superior prior to the arrival in the late 1940s of sea lamprey. In 1930, Mr. Lindquist moved to Grand Marais with his parents, Emil "Fritz" and Jenny, when he was a baby.

Special thanks to our primary sources who graciously consented to multiple oral history interviews so we could learn from people who really lived the early days of Grand Marais.

Mr. Lindquist talks with Story Scout Maddy about a pet blind fawn he had as boy in Grand Marais.

Linnea interviews Joyce and Gordon Lindquist. Joyce started Cook County's first kindergarten in 1953.

Our two-at-a-time research trip to Cook County History Museum. Story Scouts Linnea and Iris were welcomed by Katie Clark, Office and Museum Manager, to conduct historical research on ice cream and fish in the archives.

ELEMENTS OF OUTDOOR BOOK CAMP:

· Stay outside

· Stay far apart — measure 6 feet with spacer noodles to help!

· Stay creative

Outdoor Book Camp maintained conoravirus safety standards by staying outside most of the time; wearing masks at all times; spacing out at all times; keeping sanitizing stations well stocked, as seen in the red cart on the porch, and reminding people to use them. To help us estimate a safe distance, we made 6-foot long "space noodles" from plumbing foam wrap we got at Buck's Hardware Store, and decorated. Good for limbo and jump rope, too!

In Outdoor Book Camp, we got back to Cook County's Norwegian roots and the Norwegian concept of friluftsliv. Pronounced FREE-loof-sliv, the word translates to "free air life", and as lived in Norway, friluftsliv prizes a culture of getting outdoors however and whenever possible. We did just that.

As entrepreneurial writers, Story Scouts raise money to fund civic betterment projects and to print their books. Lemonade stands are one way to do it!

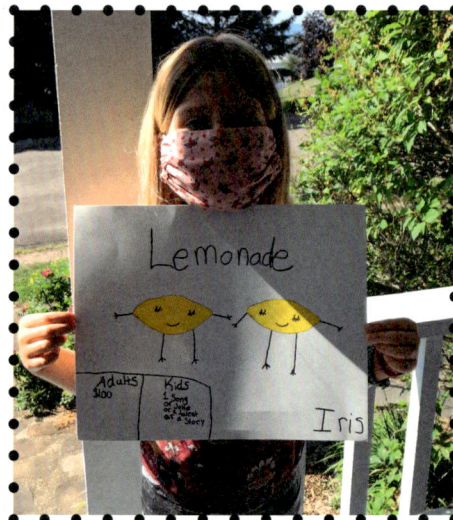

LAKE SUPERIOR SHAPE POEM

Illustration by Lily C.

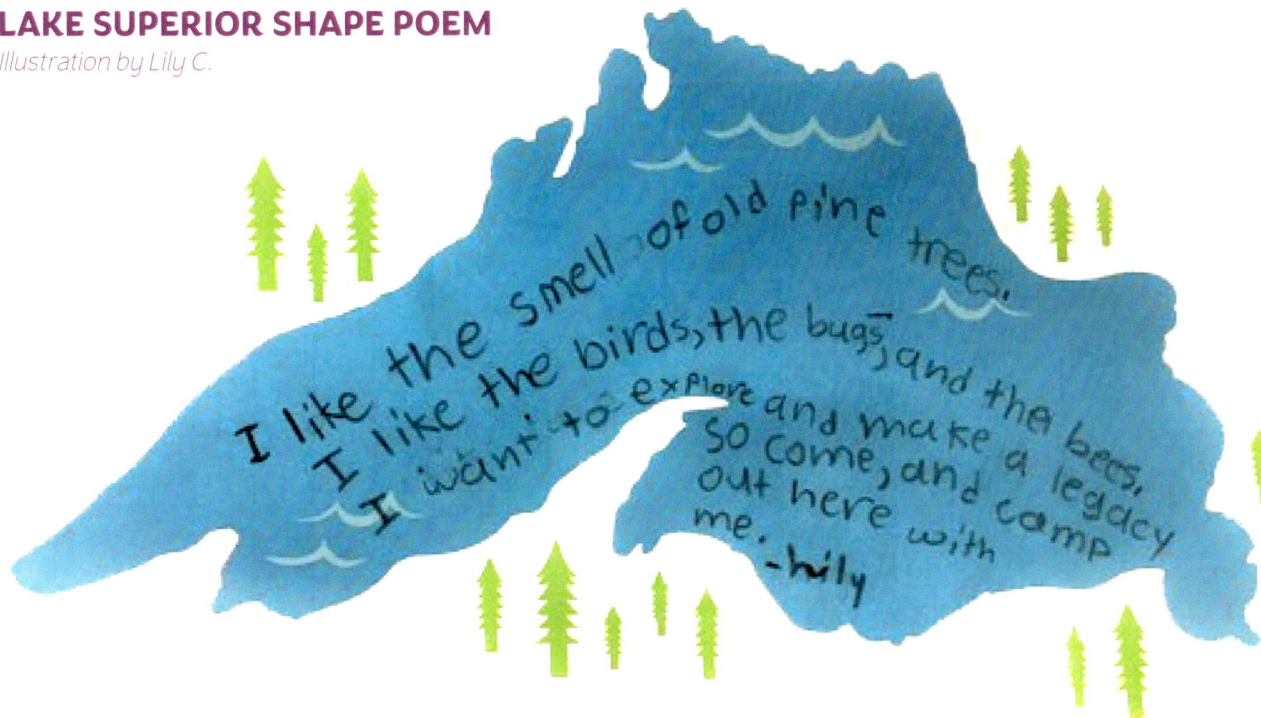

I like the smell of old pine trees,
I like the birds, the bugs, and the bees,
I want to explore and make a legacy
so come, and camp
out here with
me. -Lily

MIRA'S STICK AND MOON ALPHABET

Proofreading by Maddy M.

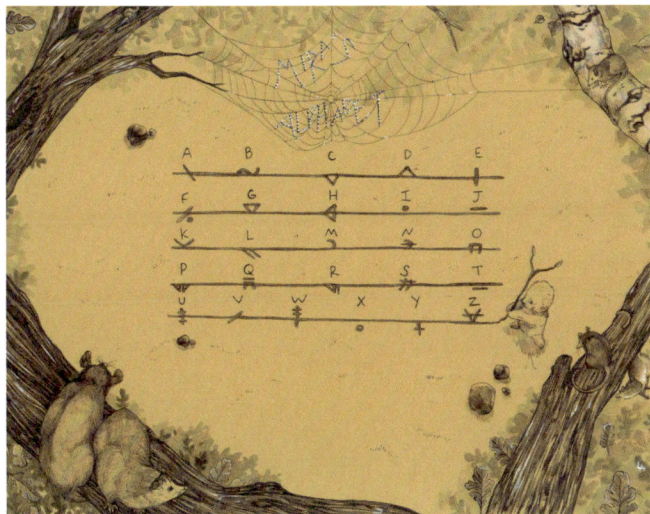

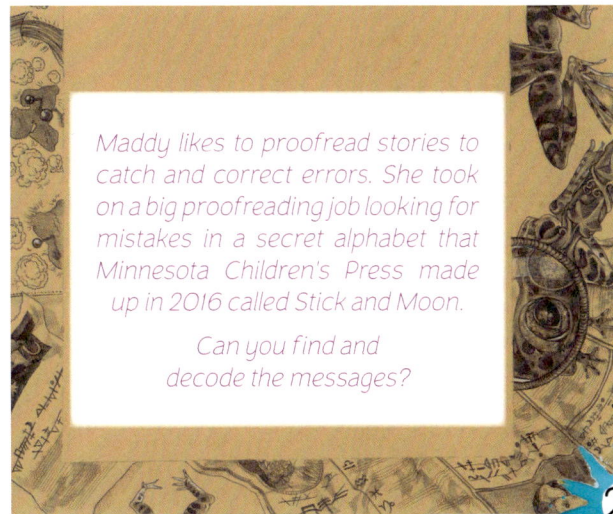

Maddy likes to proofread stories to catch and correct errors. She took on a big proofreading job looking for mistakes in a secret alphabet that Minnesota Children's Press made up in 2016 called Stick and Moon.

Can you find and decode the messages?

Part VI:
Artists' Statements

Linnea Ljosenvoor

Linnea R. Ljosenvoor is twelve years old and this is her first book. But there are several more still in the creative process in her imagination. During the pandemic she has had plenty of time to work on them. When she is not writing, she enjoys acting, reading and Lego building.

Iris Works

Iris Works is ten years old and loves animals and nature. She writes, "My favorite color is blue. I have a baby brother, and he is so cute. I like doing handstands and cartwheels and the splits. I hope to be able to finish a back bend and a walking handstand. And I hate COVID-19. It made 4th grade really hard and I miss my friends."

Sammie Garrity

Sammie is in the 10th grade where her favorite subjects are English and history. She prefers writing editorials or feature stories, and drawing to illustrate complex ideas. After the pandemic the first thing she will do is "hug all of my friends and family because it has been almost six months since I have done that." In the future, Sammie would like to be a traveling journalist or investigative reporter whose coverage spans the globe and gives people a voice when they otherwise wouldn't have one.

Lily C.

Lily is in 4th grade and likes to write and draw because it's fun to make cartoons and write books when you can make a story with anything you want to happen. After the pandemic, she is going to see all her friends and go to places like movie theaters and amusement parks.

Maddy M.

Maddy is in 6th grade and helped proofread the stories in this book. She likes drawing, writing, copy editing, proofreading, and reading "Shakespearean Insults" out loud (you can hear a clip on our website www.minnchildpress.org) and just generally being creative. The first thing she will do when the pandemic is over: "Have a big sleepover with all my friends."

26

Let the light shine!

Let the light shine!

light
ne!

Let the light shine!

Let the light shine!

Let the light shine!